TEACH ME HOW TO PRAY

Practical Applications that will Pivot your Prayers

A foundational approach to 21st Century Prayer

Journal Included

Rochelle Washington Scott

Targeted Prayer Strategies
Practical Applications that will Pivot your Prayers

Rochelle Washington Scott

Royal Kingdom Publishing

Royal Kingdom
PUBLISHING

Rochelle Washington Scott
rwashingtonscott@gmail.com

Contents

Preface

This book is for anyone who is looking to delve deeper into their faith practice through prayer. It is for those who are looking for a way to connect with God, and to find peace and comfort in their spiritual life. This book offers practical applications that will help you pivot your prayers to be more effective, meaningful, and impactful. Through the exercises provided, you will learn how to create a prayer practice that works for you and will help you to stay connected with God. This book provides guidance on how to find the right words for your prayers, how to connect with God, and how to better understand the purpose of prayer. Prayer can be an amazing tool for connecting with God and finding peace and comfort in your spiritual life. It can also help you to strengthen your faith and to be more mindful of the presence of God. With the guidance provided in this book, you will be able to use prayer to create a connection with God and to find peace and comfort in your spiritual life. I hope you find this book helpful and that it offers you the guidance you need to create a meaningful and impactful prayer practice.

Rochelle Washington Scott
Author

Chapter One

THE RELEVANCE OF PRAYER

*Let me define prayer for you in this show.
Prayer is man giving God permission or
license to interfere in earth's affairs. In
other words, prayer is earthly license
for heavenly interference.*
—MYLES MUNROE

In the 21st Century prayer has taken a dramatic shift. When we look at historical and cultural accounts, prayer was a constant in the lives of families. From praying at the dinner table to nightly prayers, prayer although ritualistic was not a foreign concept in faith-based communities. Webster's Dictionary defines prayer as "an address (such as a petition) to God or a god in word or thought." This definitely has become the driving concept when prayer is mentioned in most arenas. Prayer is thought of as a time where human beings use words to ask or make requests for what they need. In Christian churches around the world, we have seen prayer used as a form of supplication in healing, deliverance and salvation. Prayer is often seen as one dimensional which places the focus on the person praying to God.

However, if one only looks at prayer as a means of supplication, then why is prayer relevant to those who have no dire needs. What place does prayer have in the lives of those who are financially free and physically whole? Let's go Deeper. I define prayer as **the technology by which earth reaches heaven and heaven reaches earth.** So when we think about prayer, this definition is more aligned to what the Bible says about prayer. Prayer is the communication point for all believers. This gives us pause to reflect on communication. Communication is between two or more entities. This alone cancels out the culture of prayer being requests only. Prayer is how we communicate to Creator God and how Creator God communicates back to us.

The gospel song "Jesus is on The Main Line" says, "Call Him up and tell Him what you want." The lyrics from this song illustrate a simplistic understanding of prayer. In the natural when one makes a phone call, the object of the call is to have a two way conversation. The caller may be calling to make a request or just to have dialogue. This is the same concept we place before us when we are communicating with God. We are using our spiritual "cellphone" to call him and have a conversation. In this conversation, the caller talks and God listens. Then God talks and the caller listens. Oh what a beautiful dance of discussion that takes place through prayer. This is the relevance of prayer for believers in the 21st Century and beyond. This is also what makes prayer in the Christian faith different from every other religion in the world. Prayer is the only means of communication that we have in the earth realm to reach the throne room of heaven.

Prayer is Needed

Luke 18:1 (KJV) states, "And he spake a parable unto them to this end, that men ought always to pray, and not to faint." In this current world the state of affairs is the worst it has ever been. Every day we hear of wars and rumors of wars, famine, murder, disease, and so much more. I can remember being a child and watching the news with my family. At that time the news was filled with information and positive spotlights intermingled with catastrophes. This is definitely not the case in 2022. I have the local news app on my phone with the alerts turned on. For the last 6 months, every single day has had at least one alert for murder or tragic vehicle accidents. The state of our world is that which easily brings stress, anxiety, depression and loss of hope. This is why we as believers must live in a constant place of prayer. Prayer is our lifeline. Prayer is what gives us daily hope and encouragement. Through prayer we can access our heavenly father knowing that He can give us prophetic insight to what we see in the natural. Through prayer we can enter into a place of calm and rest in the presence of the almighty God. Through prayer we can develop a divine intimacy that releases peace that passes human understanding. This is the relevance of prayer.

Prayer is Multifaceted

Prayer has a variety of attributes and purposes. For the purpose of this book, I want to outline a few for our common under-standing and language.

Intimacy

First, prayer provides intimacy for human beings and Creator God. Communication remains at surface level when you do not have a deep relationship with the one with whom you are communicating. Intimacy alludes to affection, confidence, friendship, communion, and understanding. Therefore, the first layer of prayer for the believer is developing this divine relationship . This causes you to make your time with God sacred and special. Whether you are dedicating time or space (which we will address in Chapter 2), you must be intentional about building intimacy with God through the place of prayer. As you are building intimacy, seek to know God through his word. This is where we bring the Bible into our prayer time. You can not have intimacy with someone you do not know.

Adoration

The second layer of prayer is adoration. This is why developing intimacy is so important in prayer and understanding who God is. This component of prayer is combined with deepening our worship with God. This is where we begin to admire and esteem our creator. This is where we glorify Yahweh. One can think of this as a never ending honeymoon phase. Oh the wonder of being able to honor our heavenly father in the place of prayer. This is a time that many believers do not dwell in. Psalm 99:5 (ESV) commands, "Exalt the Lord our God; worship at his footstool! Holy is he!" Psalm 29:2 (ESV) reads, "Ascribe to the Lord the glory due to his name; worship the Lord in the splendor of holiness." The Word of God has multiple places that challenges us to adore our Creator.

There is something about this space in prayer that invokes an atmosphere that causes the presence of God to enter a prayer closet, room, or car. This time of reverence takes the focus off of the current realities of life and puts it on God, our constant supreme being.

Gratitude

In addition, gratitude is the third component of prayer that truly causes a perspective change . Think about it. You are in your place of prayer and all you do for ten minutes is thank the Lord. Do you know how that opens up the floodgates of heaven on your behalf ? As God's son or daughter, having a thankful heart posture should always be a priority in prayer. 1 Thessalonians 5:18 (ESV) tells us, "Give thanks in all circumstances; for this is the will of God in Christ Jesus for you." This determines that no matter what else we have to express in prayer we always preface it in a time of prayer. It is nothing like someone showing you gratitude for what you have already done for them before piling on more requests. Hebrews 12:28 reminds us to be grateful for receiving a kingdom that can not be shaken. This alone is a powerful concept that gratitude keeps us in remembrance that our kingdom is not of this world.

Repentance

Repentance is vital to keep believers humble in prayer. We must always remember that we are the creation and imperfect without the hand of God. Therefore, we must step into the place of acknowledging and repenting for anything we have done against the will of God intentionally and unknowingly. First, prayer provides intimacy for human beings and Creator God. Revelation only comes after repentance. Therefore, repentance releases the funnel of heavenly downloads. I believe that the spirit of repentance needs to be introduced to the body of Christ along with sanctification. This time in prayer allows for you to release unforgiveness, bitterness, jealousy, pride, and things of the flesh which allows Holy Spirit to have free flow in prayer. Matthew 3:8 (ESV) reminds us to, "Bear fruit in keeping with repentance."

Supplication

Now we can dive into what most believers and unbelievers think about when they focus on prayer. Most consider that prayer is equivalent to making requests or supplication. This is correct but can not be done without what we have already mentioned. 2 Chronicles 7:14 says, "If my people who are called by my name, will humble themselves, and pray and seek my face and turn from their wicked ways, then I will hear from heaven and will forgive their sin and heal their land." This lets us know that our supplication is contingent upon our posture of repentance. God will only answer when we are truly in right standing with him. Supplication is a very powerful avenue in prayer. According to Philippians 4:6 (ESV),"Do not be anxious about anything, but in every-thing by prayer and supplication with thanksgiving let your requests be made known to God." This reminds us that God actually wants to hear our petitions in conjunction with our thanksgiving. Do you see how even in prayer God requires order?

Intercession

Intercession is a powerful weapon for kingdom believers. When you cry out on behalf of someone or their situation, there is a power that is released. 1 Timothy 2:1-5 exhorts us to pray for others: "I urge, then, first of all, that requests, prayers, intercession and thanksgiving be made for everyone - for kings and all those in authority, that we may live peaceful and quiet lives in all godliness and holiness. This is good, and pleases God our Savior, who wants all men to be saved and to come to a knowledge of the truth." Intercession is what pleases our Father. Even Jesus, the greatest intercessor of all time, modeled this for us during his time on earth. Here are some of His prayers:

Jesus prayed for Peter - Luke 22:32 says, "But I have prayed for you, Simon, that your faith may not fail. And when you have turned back, strengthen your brothers." Jesus prayed for those who crucified Him. Luke 23:34 says, "Jesus said, 'Father, forgive them, for they do not know what they are doing.' And they divided up his clothes by casting lots." Jesus prayed for His disciples and for believers throughout eternity in John 17. Intercession is something as believers that we must do for our marriages, families, friends, community, churches, and our nation. We cannot sit idly by while the devil and his kingdom causes havoc and chaos.

Reception

The final layer of prayer that I will mention is reception. Reception is the part that is often overlooked and yet most vital. Reception should be done in conjunction with all prayer types. There is one question that shifts you into reception. Father God, what do you have to say? We see a model of this when Samuel was first called by God in 1 Samuel 3:1. Samuel was in training under Eli. Therefore, he was not foreign to the concept of prayer. However, the scripture goes on to tell us that, at some point Samuel had to realize that God was trying to speak to him. Eli told Samuel to respond to the voice of God by saying, "Speak Lord, for your servant is listening." Many of us need to add this phrase into our time of prayer. Remember, God wants to be a part of this conversation by way of Holy Spirit. Sometimes we leave our prayer time with no direction because we haven't given God time to reply. We have done all the talking with no active and intentional listening. The next time you go into prayer be intentional and take a notebook. This places the expectation that God will speak.

Prayer is Relevant

As you transition through the remainder of this book, you will receive language and strategies for pivoting from wherever you currently are in prayer. However, it is vital that you remain grounded in what is the foundation of prayer. The bottom line is that as a believer we cannot thrive without prayer.

Practical Application

Pause and reflect on the multiple layers of prayer discussed in Chapter 1. Which layers are you not being consistent and disciplined in? What can you do today to shift in the place of prayer?

_____

_____

_____

_____

_____

_____

_____

_____

_____

_____

_____

_____

_____

_____

_____

Chapter Two

PLANNING TIME TO PRAY

Much praying is not done because we do not plan to pray.
We do not drift into spiritual life; we do not drift into
disciplined prayer. We will not grow in prayer unless we
plan to pray. That means we must self-consciously
set aside time to do nothing but pray.

—D.A. CARSON

Where has the time gone? There are just not enough hours in the day. It was just January and now the year is almost over. The aforementioned statements are heard often in random conversations. Time has intensified over the last 20 years. Although there are still 24 hours in a day, time appears to have gotten faster. Between 5G and increased wifi speed, everything operates on overdrive. This is why it is more imperative than ever for the modern Christian believer to make planning prayer a priority. Some of our lives are so busy that if we don't schedule in our prayer times prayer will not exist in our lives. Of course we have times where prayer is spontaneous. However, for what we learned about prayer in Chapter 1, we must protect that sacred time.

Daily Prayer

Daily prayer should be scheduled at least every morning. Think about this time as a part of your sacred morning routine. Practically calculate how much time is used for your current routine inclusive of showering, brushing teeth, breakfast, etc. Then back it up by 30 minutes. This addition to your morning will cause your day to start off focused and with alignment.

Psalm 5:3 (ESV) proclaims, "O Lord, in the morning you hear my voice; in the morning I prepare a sacrifice for you to watch." The psalmist believed that the Lord would hear him and respond quickly in the early morning hours. He believed that disciplined early morning prayer placed God first in everything that needed to be accomplished for the day. He considered it a sacrifice that was equivalent to that of offering incense to the Father. Think about how sweet it is to God when we give him the first fruit of our day. Before the hustle and bustle we stop to communicate with him. Daily morning prayer yields time to ask God what assignments He has for your day. The Bible tells us in Proverbs 19:21, "Many are the plans in a person's heart, but it is the Lord's purpose that prevails." Therefore our agendas, calendars and timelines do not outweigh God's purpose for our lives. This is why we must ask every morning for God to order our steps.

Another time to add daily prayer is when you close out your day in the night season. Praying at the end of your day is a way to thank the Lord for all that he has afforded you throughout the day. Just as you add 30 minutes for morning prayer, you will do the same for night prayers. This time is special for releasing the peace of God before falling asleep. During this time your spirit can be revived as your body and soul prepares for rest. During this time your prayer consists of scriptures like 2 Timothy 1:7, "For God's not given me a spirit of fear, but a spirit of love and of power and a sound mind." During this time you decree the Shepherd's prayer from Psalm 23. During night prayers, one can also pray about rest and sleep. Exodus 33:14, "And he said, My presence will go with you, and I will give you rest." Matthew 11:28-30 says, "Come to me, all who labor and are heavy laden, and I will give you rest. Take my yoke upon you, and learn from me, for I am gentle and lowly in heart, and you will find rest for your souls. For my yoke is easy, and my burden is light." Psalm 4:8 reads, "In peace I will both lie down and sleep; for you alone, O Lord, make me dwell in safety." These aforementioned scriptures are a few of many that can jumpstart you in the place of night time prayers.

It often baffles me at how Christianity is the only religion that struggles in the discipline of planning and implementing prayer. Muslims have five daily prayer times, and they are considered one of their faith's most important disciplines. Not only do they have the dedicated time but also the assigned rituals for each time. They are taught to prepare their mind and body before entering into a time of prayer. From dress to cleanliness to an assigned prayer place, Muslims are very devout in prayer. Jewish law mandates that Jews pray three times a day. This consists of a morning prayer, afternoon prayer, and evening prayer. Historically, Jews even had to pray in a specific direction. There are many more examples. However, I believe you get the point.

As believers we shout and dance about a Savior who is alive and well. Yet we spend the least amount of time meeting with him. In the times we are living we need to plan for prayer like never before. Find a dedicated time that works for where you are in life. If you are married, plan for time to pray with your spouse. If you have children, plan family prayer time. Prayer is vital to your survival. Therefore, treat it as a dose of medication that you can not miss. Set timers. Create an atmosphere that is conducive for your dedicated time. Bring all your resources (Bible, journal, pens, instrumental worship music).

Practical Application

Take out your planner or scheduler. Reflect on where you can plan prayer in your daily schedule. Add the time as an appointment on your calendar. Track it with fidelity.

_____

_____

_____

_____

_____

_____

_____

_____

_____

_____

_____

_____

_____

_____

_____

_____

Chapter Three
THE PRAYER WATCHES

Take ye heed, watch and pray:
for ye know not when the time is. Mark 13:33
—JESUS

Luke 18:1 begins with Jesus talking in a parable. The scripture says, "And he spake a parable unto them to this end, that men ought always to pray, and not to faint." Jesus was explaining to the people that prayer is a constant and should be done with fervency. Many Christians are not aware that every hour of the day is a part of a specific prayer watch. This is important to know because it helps one identify their prayer assignment based upon the time of day or night they are called to pray. Prayer watches are pivotal in the life of every believer. This is not just a subject for those who are just coming into the knowledge of Jesus Christ,but also for those who have been called to be watchmen and gatekeepers. It is important that the kingdom believers get back on their post in the power of prayer. It is time for intercessors to pick up the burden of prayer. Revival is coming to the land but only through the place of prayer. Habakkuk 2:11 states, "I will stand upon my watch, and set me upon the tower, and will watch to see what he will say unto me, and what I shall answer when I am reproved." Every believer has at least one prayer watch that you are assigned to. Sometimes the watch may change based on your season in life. However, when we begin to see a lot of demonic activity during a specific time, it is because the watchmen have abandoned the post.

The Role of the Watchman In ancient times, the watchman was responsible for detecting and deterring any possible threats to the city. This included safeguarding against military invasions as well as any other potential intrusions. Moreover, the watchman was expected to alert the citizens if any danger was imminent, as instructed by God. According to Ezekiel 33:6, the watchman would be held accountable for any deaths that occurred due to their failure to warn the people. Some characteristics of a Watchman: the watchman must be able to observe their surroundings, possess a certain level of knowledge, and speak up against any injustices they encounter. Additionally, they must remain vigilant, sober and alert at all times, while also following God's will and direction.

The watchman must also be faithful and obedient, fully devoted to the Lord and committed to fulfilling His plans and purposes. As the Psalmist wrote, "I will lift up my eyes to the hills. Where does my help come from? My help comes from the Lord, the Maker of heaven and earth." (Psalm 121:1-2). In the same way, the watchman must look to the Lord for guidance and strength in their calling. The Apostle Paul reminds us in Colossians 4:2, to "Continue steadfastly in prayer, being watchful in it with thanksgiving." As watchmen, we must be continually aware and pray for our families, churches, and nation. We must not limit our watch to the enemy's activity, but we must also watch for and recognize the manifestation of God's plans and purposes. The following is a breakdown of all 8 prayer watches.

The First Night Watch (6:00 PM-9:00 PM)

This watch is a time of meditation. During this watch it is vital to have the Word of God as a point of reference. This time is a time for divine judgements, deliverance, resurrection, and to come against demonic systems. In Matthew 14:15-23, Jesus used the first night watch to go aside and pray after he had performed miracles and ministered to the crowds. The bible says Jesus went up on the mountain alone in the evening to pray. For the believer this watch is a time of quiet reflection and receiving clear directions from the Lord without the clutter and noise of the day.

This is also the watch to pray for divine healing. Mark 1:32 says, "That evening at sundown they brought to him all who were sick or oppressed by demons." Luke 4:40 reads, " Now when the sun was setting, all those who had any who were sick with various diseases brought them to him, and he laid his hands on every one of them and healed them." During this watch, this is the time to pull on heaven for miracles and breaking of strongholds. One can think of this watch as the foundation watch that sets the tone for the remainder of the night and the beginning of all the watches. Therefore, this is also the time to make decrees and declarations over yourself, family, neighborhood, city, church, and nation. For it is in this watch that we are decreeing the word of God and possessing the gates!

The Second Night Watch (9:00 PM -12:00 AM)

The second night watch is a time for thanksgiving and favor. In Exodus we see how the Israelites received the favor of God even before midnight. Even before their deliverance, the Lord provided them with everything they would need to successfully leave out of bondage during this time of the night. Exodus 12:35-36, "And the people of Israel did as Moses had instructed; they asked the Egyptians for clothing and articles of silver and gold. The Lord caused the Egyptians to look favorably on the Israelites, and they gave the Israelites whatever they asked for. So they stripped the Egyptians of their wealth!" During this time, we must pray for the favor of God and man.

This is also the watch of revelation and impartation. Luke 12:37-38 says, "Blessed are those servants whom the master, when he comes, will find watching. Assuredly, I say to you that he will gird himself and have them sit down to eat, and will come and serve them. And if he should come in the second watch, or come in the third watch, and find them so, blessed are those servants." There is something about those intercessors who are called to this watch that have a true hunger for a deeper understanding of the word of God. If that has been your desire this is the watch to come with your bible and journal. Ask the Lord to give you deeper revelation and understanding of his word during this time.

The Third Night Watch (12:00 AM-3:00 AM)

This watch is the most important watch of the night when it comes to spiritual warfare . It is during this watch that the demonic activity is at its highest peak. This is the watch for those who are called to come against witchcraft, warfare, principalities, and violators in the spirit realm. Judges 16:3 says, "But Samson lay there only until the middle of the night. Then he got up and took hold of the doors of the city gate, together with the two posts, and tore them loose, bar and all. He lifted them to his shoulders and carried them to the top of the hill that faces Hebron." It was at midnight that Samson took his strength back and declared war on the enemy. The midnight hour is not the hour of quiet prayer. This is the hour of intense prayer. Acts 16:25-26 says, "But at midnight Paul and Silas were praying and singing hymns to God, and the prisoners were listening to them. Suddenly there was a great earthquake, so that the foundations of the prison were shaken; and immediately all the doors were opened and everyone's chains were loosed." Worship and warfare are spiritual twins. You can not have one without the other. The way to combat the enemy is through your worship and your warfare during this watch. Whatever you are warring against, put a praise on it! Psalm 119:62 tells us to rise at midnight and give thanks to God because of his righteous judgements. Therefore, we go into this watch warring and worshipping with the expectation that almighty God is about to show out on our behalf!

The Fourth Night Watch (3:00AM - 6:00AM)

Lamentations 3:22-23 reads, "Because of the Lord's great love we are not consumed, for his compassions never fail. They are new every morning; great is your faithfulness." This watch is where you can decree the mercies of God. During this watch you can command your day with prophetic decrees and declaring God's word. This is also a time for divine revelation. This is why it is vital to have a journal and pen to record what God is speaking during this watch. During this watch you want to sit quietly for a time to receive downloads and blueprints by way of Holy Spirit.

The fourth watch of the night is an important time because this is when the Lord delivers us from the bondage of the enemy. This is the time when Jesus walked on the water to help the disciples who were caught in the storm (Matthew 14:25-33). This is the time to declare God's Word and break every yoke of bondage that would attempt to hinder His will for our lives to manifest. Psalm 19:2 says "Day unto day utters speech, and night unto night reveals knowledge." This is the time to establish the course of our day by speaking God's Word. When we pray during this time, we are claiming victory in the morning. The Lord will hear our prayers and send His angels to work on our behalf. We will be protected and our enemies will scatter in seven directions.This watch is when we begin to cry out for the mercy of God.

Start the Day with Prayer

Matthew 24:43 tells us to be vigilant and be aware of the enemy's plans and tactics. This is a prayerful watch that entrusts the day to the Lord and allows the angels to do their work. Pray that the enemy's plans and strategies will be rendered powerless and that the day will be filled with prosperity, blessing, and favor. Prepare for the day by affirming the Lord's plans and purpose for your life and enforcing them over Satan's. Declare that no weapon formed against you will prosper and that all who speak against you will be proven wrong. Ask for protection and for the Lord to defeat your enemies and scatter them in seven directions. Be confident that the Lord will go before you and make your way smooth and successful.

Invoking the Lord's Word this is a time for celestial activity or interference and a time for blessings from above. When we call on Him, the Lord listens to our requests and dispatches His messengers to work in our favor. Dedicate all of the work for the day and ask for protection for God's people all through the day. "You will pray to Him and He will listen to you; you will carry out your vows. You will also speak out a thing and it will be established for you; so will your light shine on your way" (Job 22:27-28). Declarations of faith for this prayer watch: Father, in Jesus' Name… You have gone before me to prepare my path, to make the crooked path straight, and to make the arduous route smooth. Father, I entrust my labor to You and You cause my plans to be successful and all that I apply myself to do succeeds (Proverbs 16:3). Father, today I have favor with everyone who looks upon me and Your favor creates a circle around me, encircling me and enveloping me like a shield. You will carry out Your plans for my life because Your faithful love lasts forever. I enforce Your plans and purpose for my life over and against the plans and purpose of Satan. Satan, the blood of Jesus is against you. You don't have any power over my life. No weapon that is used against me will succeed, and anyone who speaks against me will be proven wrong because my vindication comes from God (Isaiah 54:17). You will prevail over my enemies; they will come against me but run away before me in seven directions! (Deuteronomy 28:7). In Jesus name Amen.

The First Day Watch (6:00AM -9:00AM)

Prayers for Spiritual Strengthening

(2 Corinthians 9:15; Ephesians 4:12) Let us ask God to strengthen us spiritually through His Holy Spirit. As we rise in the morning and the sun begins to shine, we can remember Malachi 4:2, which speaks of the Lord's healing and restoring power. We can pray that He blesses us with His loving-kindness, pour out His tender mercies, and forgive all of our sins. As we step out into the day, we can ask the Holy Spirit to equip us with the strength and power to do all that He has called us to do. We can also plead the Blood of Jesus over ourselves and against any physical, mental, or emotional abuse, diseases, viruses, and illnesses that would try to overtake us. We can trust that He will keep us in perfect health all the days of our life, and that He will redeem us from the hands of the devil.

The Second Day Watch (9:00AM -12:00PM)

The second prayer watch of the day, or the third hour, falls between 9 am and 12 pm. This is when we should be actively carrying out our intended roles in life. Most labor begins at 9 am or earlier, and being unproductive at this hour is considered idleness. The Garden of Gethsemane was the place where Jesus prayed at dawn, and it is just before 9 am that His earnest pleas were answered. For our benefit, Jesus had to suffer the heavy burden of the cross, and in His petition, He stated: "Abba, Father, he cried out," everything is possible for you. Please take this cup of suffering away from me. Yet I want your will to be done, not mine." (Mark 14:35-36)

At the third hour of 9 am Jesus was crucified and died for our sins. This was the ultimate act of love and sacrifice for us and it is what will save us from our sins. During this hour, we are called to reflect on the love of Jesus and to remember why he died. As we reflect on the cross and the atoning work of Christ, we should strive to live a crucified life in his likeness. This is the time to remember our calling and purpose on this earth, and to strive to be more like Jesus in our actions and words.

The Third Day Watch (12:00PM-3:00PM)

During the prayer watch from noon to 3pm, this is the time of day that is said to be the most intense and powerful. During this period, the sun is at its peak and this is the time of judgment and guidance. It is a time to shake the foundations and to call on God for deliverance from wickedness and evil. During This Third Prayer Watch Pray For: Taking refuge in the shadow of the Almighty this is the time to petition for refuge under the shadow of the Almighty. Call on the Most High to be your shelter and your safe haven from any calamity that may come your way. Pray for safety and security as you seek the refuge of God, the Most High. Lastly, pray for divine guidance.

This prayer watch is a time to ask for divine guidance on all matters concerning you, your family, your business and your ministry. Ask for the eyes of understanding to be enlightened, for wisdom to be granted and for the knowledge of God to come to you. Ask for divine direction on the decisions you are faced with and the paths that you need to choose. James 1:5 states, "If any of you lack wisdom, you should ask God, who gives generously to all without finding fault, and it will be given to you."

Scriptures For Midday

John 4:6 Jacob's well was there; and Jesus, tired from the long walk, sat wearily beside the well about noontime.

Matthew 27:45 "The Death of Jesus" At noon, darkness fell across the whole land until three o'clock.

Acts 26:13 About noon, Your Majesty, as I was on the road, a light from heaven brighter than the sun shone down on me and my companions.

Jeremiah 15:8 There will be more widows than the grains of sand on the seashore. At noontime I will bring a destroyer against the mothers of young men. I will cause anguish and terror to come upon them suddenly.

Job 11:13-20 If only you would prepare your heart and lift up your hands to him in prayer! Get rid of your sins, and leave all iniquity behind you. Then your face will brighten with innocence. You will be strong and free of fear. You will forget your misery; it will be like water flowing away. Your life will be brighter than the noonday. Even darkness will be as bright as morning. Having hope will give you courage. You will be protected and will rest in safety. You will lie down unafraid, and many will look to you for help. But the wicked will be blinded. They will have no escape. Their only hope is death.

Psalm 91:1-8 Those who live in the shelter of the Most High will find rest in the shadow of the Almighty. This I declare about the Lord: He alone is my refuge, my place of safety; he is my God, and I trust him. For he will rescue you from every trap and protect you from deadly disease. He will cover you with his feathers. He will shelter you with his wings. His faithful promises are your armor and protection. Do not be afraid of the terrors of the night, nor the arrow that flies in the day. Do not dread the disease that stalks in darkness, nor the disaster that strikes at midday. Though a thousand fall at your side, though ten thousand are dying around you, these evils will not touch you. Just open your eyes, and see how the wicked are punished.

Psalm 37:5-6 Commit your way to the Lord, Trust also in Him, And He shall bring it to pass. He shall bring forth your righteousness as the light, And your justice as the noonday.

The Fourth Day Watch (3:00PM-6:00PM)

This is the last watch of the day, symbolizing new beginnings. We rejoice in the power of the Cross, which reminds us of Christ's willingness to die for us and of His great love. This watch is a time of self-sacrifice, revival, and rejoicing. During this watch you should dedicate yourself to the service of God. During this watch you pray against anything that causes you to not be committed to your kingdom assignment. This is the watch where you ask God to send your divine connections and connectors.

Hebrews 13:20-21, "Now may the God of peace who brought up our Lord Jesus from the dead, that great Shepherd of the sheep, through the blood of the everlasting covenant, make you complete in every good work to do His will, working in you what is well pleasing in His sight, through Jesus Christ, to whom be glory forever and ever. Amen."

John 15:13, "Greater love has no one than this: to lay down one's life for one's friends."

Practical Application

Now that you have a deeper understanding in the prayer watches, where has God been signaling you to go deeper in prayer? Are there times that you are awakened out of sleep and not sure why? Are there certain times in the day where you feel an overwhelming urge to pray? Began to press into those times using the prayer targets as a guide to a deeper place with God.

_____

_____

_____

_____

_____

_____

_____

_____

_____

_____

_____

_____

_____

Chapter Four
TARGETED PRAYER STRATEGIES

Prayer is the portal that brings the power of heaven down to earth. It is kryptonite to the enemy and to all his plots against you.
—PRISCILLA SHIRER

Luke 11:1 tells the reader, "One day Jesus was praying in a certain place. When he finished, one of his disciples said to him, "Lord, teach us to pray, just as John taught his disciples." This verse is a blatant reminder that there is an ever evolving methodology to prayer. For Jesus did not use the same method to teach as John did. As a matter of fact Jesus used the **Our Father Prayer** model to teach his disciples the principles of prayer based on who he was.

Jesus' Prayer

Many churches and Christians teach and call the prayer that Jesus used "The Our Father Model Prayer". Therefore, in the church world, it has become a ritualistic prayer that we pray out of religion. We simply miss most of the concepts that Jesus was trying to teach and model for his disciples. As a matter of fact most people consider as Jesus' answer to the disciples petition is the following:

Luke 11:2-4 And he said unto them, When ye pray, say, Our Father which art in heaven, Hallowed be thy name. Thy kingdom come. Thy will be done, as in heaven, so in earth. Give us day by day our daily bread. And forgive us our sins; for we also forgive every one that is indebted to us. And lead us not into temptation; but deliver us from evil.

You see, the emphasis of the prayer was the strategy. There were specific principles in the prayer that Jesus wanted his disciples to understand. Jesus was not just teaching the disciples a prayer. For they were aware of prayer in their culture because even the Pharisees prayed. The disciples asked for **the how** because there was an intimacy that Jesus demonstrated in prayer that they had never observed. The first strategy was to recognize and give honor to God whom they were praying to. Jesus was reminding the disciples to always acknowledge the holiness of the father first in prayer. Jesus also demonstrated acknowledging that it was all about God's kingdom, God's will, and God's name. Think about this for a minute. If you spend time at the beginning of prayer focused on God and not what he can do for you, the perspective of your heart and mind in prayer shifts. Oh, that we would return to bringing glory to God in our prayers. Another strategy in the model was to pray for the will of God to manifest. Very similar to what Jesus said before dying in Luke 22:42, "Father, if thou be willing, remove this cup from me: nevertheless not my will, but thine, be done." Jesus showed us no matter what the situation modeled to always return to the will of God not our own.

In addition we see the strategy of praying for our daily physical needs. This shows how God really cares about the physical state of man. 1 Corinthians 6:19, "Or do you not know that your body is a temple of the Holy Spirit who is in you, whom you have from God, and that you are not your own?" This also shows that we are to constantly rely on God for direction in our needs being met regardless of our current resources or reserves. Jesus continues to model but shifts to repentance. However, this is a child of God asking forgiveness. This causes us to acknowledge that we are in continuous need of the grace of God. We must always deal with the problem of personal sin in the posture of prayer. Jesus added a caveat by saying that we must forgive others just as we expect to be forgiven by our Father. Therefore, even in prayer, we must release unforgiveness. We cannot pray from a spirit of offense. Jesus even taught us to pray against temptation. This is vital for it requires the believer to inquire for the protection and guidance from God.

Everything that I mentioned is often not acknowledged as the rationale of the model of prayer that Jesus provided. However, what's even more astounding, is that many believers leave out the remainder of the chapter. The remainder of the chapter was the actual teaching that the disciples asked for. Jesus taught of the amazing grace of God when we come to him in prayer. God is never too busy to hear from his children no matter the hour of the day. He is not a God that causes his children to suffer or lack. That's why we are told to ask, seek, and knock. God will answer those whom he loves.

Reflect on how Jesus modeled and explained the strategy of prayer. Sometimes as believers we are not receiving answers or hearing God because we are praying amiss. James 4:3 "All of you ask, and receive not, because all of you ask amiss, that all of you may consume it upon your lusts." When we have no strategy in prayer, we end up praying in the soulish realm. Our soul is our mind, will, and emotions. Therefore, when we pray in the soulish realm, our prayers come from what we feel, what we want, and what we know. This is in direct contradiction to praying to the will of God. James 5:16b tells us that "The effectual fervent prayer of a righteous man availeth much." Targeted prayer strategies are strategies that are effective, productive, constructive, powerful, worthwhile, potent, and fruitful. Let's take a look at some strategies.

Targeted Prayer Strategy #1

This first prayer strategy works when you are praying for a specific topic or focus such as your finances or health. The first step is to write out the prayer focus/topic. Try to be as specific as possible. Next, define the prayer focus. Literally, look it up in the dictionary. In addition, research scriptures about the prayer focus. Add these scriptures to your journal along with your definition. I suggest finding at least 3 scriptures. Once you have read and written your scriptures, highlight prayer points from the scriptures that you should pray. Then, ask the Holy Spirit if he has additional words and points for your topic. Listen and write! Finally, pray! (See addendum document A for example)

Targeted Prayer Strategy #2

This second prayer strategy is one to build your tool box so that you are prepared in the place of prayer. Oftentimes, we are not able to stretch our vocabulary in prayer because we have not studied the word of God concerning a variety of issues. Earlier, I told you to always take a journal into your prayer time. Part of this should be dedicated to preparation of prayer. Make a list of common prayer targets. Leave room to add as you begin to go deeper in prayer. Similar to strategy #1, find scriptures pertaining to that topic. Ask yourself two questions. What did you learn from the scriptures? What is God saying by way of the Holy Spirit? Mark these pages and refer to them when there is a call to pray. Use the following examples.

Pray for God's protection (Psalm 91:14-16): "Because he loves me," says the Lord, "I will rescue him; I will protect him, for he acknowledges my name. He will call on me, and I will answer him; I will be with him in trouble, I will deliver him and honor him. With long life I will satisfy him and show him my salvation."

Pray for God's guidance (Psalm 25:4-5): "Show me your ways, Lord, teach me your paths. Guide me in your truth and teach me, for you are God my Savior, and my hope is in you all day long."

Pray for spiritual strength (Ephesians 6:10-11): "Finally, be strong in the Lord and in his mighty power. Put on the full armor of God, so that you can take your stand against the devil's schemes."

Pray for discernment (Hebrews 4:12): "For the word of God is alive and active. Sharper than any double-edged sword, it penetrates even to dividing soul and spirit, joints and marrow; it judges the thoughts and attitudes of the heart."

Pray for the power of the Holy Spirit (Luke 11:13): "If you then, though you are evil, know how to give good gifts to your children, how much more will your Father in heaven give the Holy Spirit to those who ask him!"

Pray for God's will to be done (Matthew 6:10): "Your kingdom come, your will be done on earth as it is in heaven."

Targeted Prayer Strategy #3

Start prayer with scriptures that adore and praise God. Don't ask Him for anything, just spend time loving Him. The Bible says that God inhabits the praises of His people. This means that as you begin to praise Him in the place of prayer He will dwell with you. Use the following scriptures to jumpstart this prayer strategy.

Psalm 18:2-3 -"Oh Lord, you are worthy of all praise. You are the king of kings, and Lord of Lords. You are my rock and my fortress. I will always worship you, Lord"

Psalm 100:4 – "Enter his gates with thanksgiving, and his courts with praise! Give thanks to him; bless his name!"

Psalm 150:2 – "Praise him for his mighty deeds; praise him according to his excellent greatness!"

Psalm 145:3 – "Great is the Lord, and greatly to be praised, and his greatness is unsearchable."

Practical Application

What was your take-away from this chapter? How will you incorporate targeted prayer strategies?

_____

_____

_____

_____

_____

_____

_____

_____

_____

_____

_____

_____

_____

_____

Chapter Five

MARRIAGE PRAYER STRATEGIES

The greatest gifts we can give each other
In marriage is to pray for one another.
—ROCHELLE SCOTT

As described first in Genesis, marriage is a God-ordained, covenant relationship between a man and a woman. Biblical marriage is meant to be a physical representation of the relationship between Christ and his bride, the Ecclesia. Matthew 19:4-6 says, "Haven't you read," Jesus replied, "that at the beginning the Creator 'made them male and female,' and said, 'For this reason a man will leave his father and mother and be united to his wife, and the two will become one flesh'? So they are no longer two, but one flesh. Therefore what God has joined together, let no one separate." This is the perfect plan of marriage from our Creator God. Yet society and the culture has attempted to change the original intent of marriage. Even now the Supreme Court has worked to change the legal definition of marriage. The enemy's agenda is to destroy the one thing that is a daily reminder of God and his love for us. This is why in the days we live in, we must pray fervently and intentionally for our marriages. We can not wait for trials and warfare to come. We must pray preventive prayers as well. How do we pray for marriages? First, start by seeing what the Bible says about kingdom marriage.

God Ordained Marriage

When we have issues with our plumbing, we call the plumber. When our body is not working properly, we call the doctor. Yet when our marriage is out of sorts we skip right over the creator and manufacturer. Above every other point that I will make in this chapter, the most important one is God created, ordained and blessed marriage. This means that everything about a kingdom marriage comes from him. "Marriage is honorable among all, and the bed undefiled" (Hebrews 13:4). How amazing is it to understand that God himself blessed marriage! He designed it to be an organism that brought joy, honor, love and so much more to humanity. Think about it. The Bible says, "The blessing of the Lord makes rich, and he adds no sorrow with it. (Proverbs 10:22)" Well since God blessed kingdom marriage, then marriage should make us rich and add no sorrow to our lives. This is such an important prayer target to add to our daily marriage declarations and decrees. The enemy has caused so much chaos and confusion in marriages. This has brought in much sorrow, lack, frustration, depression, confusion and much more into marriages. But we refuse to bow down to his tactics! As kingdom believers, we will echo what God says about our marriages. Pause here and look for other scriptures that echo what God has decreed over marriages. Write those scriptures down with a prayer declaration/decree for each. Announce these daily over your marriage.

Oneness

As stated earlier in Matthew 19:4-6, Creator God made man and woman to become one flesh that should not be separated. This gives us our first prayer point for marriage. We must pray for oneness in our marriage. The Merriam Webster dictionary defines oneness as the quality or state or fact of being one: such as wholeness, harmony, unity, identity and integrity. When we look at the word of God, there are several scriptures that line up with this definition. Romans 12:16 tell us to "Live in harmony with one another. Do not be proud, but be willing to associate with people of low position. Do not be conceited." So our prayer would be: Lord, help my spouse and I to live in harmony with one another. Let us be willing to submit to each other as unto you. Colossians 3:14 reads, "And over all these virtues put on love, which binds them all together in perfect unity." Prayer: Lord, let my spouse and I put on love daily as a garment that we may be tied together in perfect unity. Pause here and look for other scriptures that connect to the definition of oneness. Write those scriptures down with a prayer for each. Pray these scriptures daily over your marriage.

Intimacy

Ephesians 5:31 (NIV), "For this reason a man will leave his father and mother and be united to his wife, and the two will become one flesh." This not only signifies oneness but also intimacy. When we think back to the Garden of Eden, God took a rib from Adam while he was asleep to form a woman. This is a representation of the intimacy of marriage. Our marriages should be so intimate that we literally feel as if we are a part of each other. We see an example of this in Psalm 139:3-4. The Passion translation reads, "You are so intimately aware of me, Lord. You read my heart like an open book and you know all the words I'm about to speak before I even start a sentence! You know every step I will take before my journey even begins." Many times I have talked to couples that have been married 25 or more years. They all have some form of this scripture to say about their spouses. This is what we should pray for even in our marriages. We need to ask our father to let our interests in our spouses bring a greater closeness. Let our hearts be open books before our spouses. This leads to praying for the posture and position of the heart. The Word of God speaks loudly in regards to the heart. Matthew 6:19-21 (NIV) commands, "Do not store up for yourselves treasures on earth, where moths and vermin destroy, and where thieves break in and steal. But store up for yourselves treasures in heaven, where moths and vermin do not destroy, and where thieves do not break in and steal. For where your treasure is, there your heart will be also." Proverbs 4:23 (NIV) warns, "Above all else, guard your heart, for everything you do flows from it." Proverbs 3:5-6 (ESV) proclaims, "Trust in the Lord with all your heart, and do not lean on your own understanding. In all your ways acknowledge him, and he will make straight your paths." Therefore, intimacy is a heart thing! If you are having problems with intimacy in your marriage, the prayer targets should be about the heart. Pause here and look for other scriptures that connect to the posture and position of the heart. Write those scriptures down with a prayer for each. Pray these scriptures daily over your marriage.

Lifelong Covenant

Kingdom marriage is a lifelong covenant. To truly understand this, let's reflect on Jesus Christ and his bride. When a person accepts Jesus as their Lord and Savior, they are now married to him as a part of the church. This is a covenant between them and Christ. It is meant to be sacred, holy, undefiled, unbreakable, everlasting and without a contingency plan. This is the same for our earthly marriages. Jesus said it this way, "So they are no longer two, but one flesh. Therefore, what God has joined together, let no one separate" (Matthew 19:6). How can you separate flesh or a body? You can't! This metaphor was used to explain the covenant of a God ordained marriage. Therefore, if our marriages are truly under God, this is also a decree and prayer that should be consistent in our lives. Take some time to study covenant according to the Word of God. Use this as a springboard to pray for the lifelong covenant of your marriage.

Heavenly Father,

We come before You on this day to ask for Your blessing and protection over our marriage. Thank You for giving us the gift of being together and for allowing us to experience the joy of being husband and wife.

We pray that You would be the foundation of our marriage, that You would be the center of our relationship. We ask that You would help us to be patient and understanding of one another, to show love and kindness to each other, and to be willing to forgive when either of us make mistakes.

We ask that You would help us to remain faithful to each other and to grow closer to You as a couple. Please give us the strength and courage to face the difficult times together and to be a source of comfort and support to one another.

We thank You for the joys that come with marriage and ask that You would help us to remain humble and grateful for all that You have given us. Please be with us and guide us each day, so that our marriage may be strong and our love may endure.

Amen

Heavenly Father,

We thank You for the gift of marriage and the blessing of spending our lives together. We ask that You would guide us in every step of our marriage, leading us in Your will and helping us to be patient and understanding with one another.

Bless us with Your grace and protection, so that we can grow closer together in love and commitment. Give us strength to persevere through the difficult times, and fill our hearts with patience, kindness, and joy.

Help us to be examples of Your love for each other and for our family. Give us the courage to always choose love and to stay committed to our marriage even when it is hard.

We thank You for Your mercy and grace and for the gift of marriage. We pray that You would continue to be at the center of our relationship, blessing us with the strength and courage to love and support each other.

In Jesus' Name,
Amen.

Practical Application

Now that we have gathered some tools for marriage prayer strategies, take some time to write a prayer for your marriage. This can be done with or without your spouse. How will you use this going forward?

_____

_____

_____

_____

_____

_____

_____

_____

_____

_____

_____

_____

_____

_____

_____

_____

Chapter Six

PARENT PRAYER STRATEGIES

You'll never be a perfect parent,
but you can be a praying parent.
—MARK BATTERSON

Parenting in today's society is definitely not for the faint of heart. The dynamics have changed dramatically over the years for a variety of reasons. However, God's order of the family has not changed. In Genesis we see God's original plan for the family. Genesis 1:28, "Be fruitful and multiply and fill the earth and subdue it, and have dominion over the fish of the sea and over the birds of the heavens and over every living thing that moves on the earth." God created man and woman to procreate and fill the earth. Just as God is our Father in heaven, we must realize that we as parents collectively are the physical representation of him to our children in the earth realm. This means just as God has given us the instructions to grow and reach our destined purpose in him; it is our assignment to do the same for our children until they are at the age of accountability.

Before we can even jump into understanding prayer strategies for our children, we must first understand what parenting truly is. Deuteronomy 6:5-9 says, " Love the Lord your God with all your heart, with all your soul, and with all your strength. Take to heart these words that I give you today. Repeat them to your children. Talk about them when you're at home or away, when you lie down or get up. Write them down, and tie them around your wrist, and wear them as headbands as a reminder. Write them on the doorframes of your houses and on your gates." Deuteronomy 11:19 reads, "And you shall teach them your children, speaking of them when thou sittest in thine house, and when thou walkest by the way, when thou liest down, and when thou risest up." Proverbs 22:6 tells us, " Train up a child in the way he should go; even when he is old he will not depart from it." Jesus says in Matthew 18:5-6, "And anyone who welcomes a little child like this on my behalf is welcoming me. But if you cause one of these little ones who trusts in me to fall into sin, it would be better for you to have a large millstone tied around your neck and be drowned in the depths of the sea." Psalm 78:2-4 says, " For I will speak to you in a parable. I will teach you hidden lessons from our past— stories we have heard and known, stories our ancestors handed down to us. We will not hide these truths from our children; we will tell the next generation about the glorious deeds of the Lord,about his power and his mighty wonders." These scriptures collectively bring true understanding to the God ordained assignment of parenting. Parents have a responsibility to their children. They are literally the facilitator of their children's lives under God. They are the excavators of what has been hidden deep within their children. Therefore, it is vital that parents pray for parenting. When is the last time that you as a parent prayed, for yourself with the focus of parenting? Have you ever fasted for parenting blueprints and strategies? Oftentimes due to the cares of life, we can take this for granted. Let's repent and recenter our parenting through prayer starting today. Use the aforementioned scriptures to help you with the following prayer target. God help me to understand my parenting assignment!

Spirit Led

First and foremost, parents must pray that they are spirit led with their children. There is no cookie cutter approach to parenting. Why? The word of the Lord tells us that we are uniquely made by God. Therefore, we must pray according to Zechariah 4:6 when it comes to parenting. Lord help us to parent not by might nor by power but by your spirit. If you have multiple children those directives from the Holy Spirit may look different for each one. For example, at the time of writing this book, I have a 14 year old son, 12 year old daughter, and a 10 year old daughter. My son has just started his journey as a high schooler. Like most boys his age, he loves gaming. He is very disciplined and is very selective of his friends. My daughters are currently homeschooled. While one loves it, my middle child absolutely would prefer to be with friends on campus. Each of my children are at different stages in their childhood journey and are experiencing a variety of emotions and struggles. Therefore, my prayer has been for God to show me how to tier my parenting according to the needs of the gifts that he has entrusted me with. This has led to me receiving spiritual intel on what to do for them collectively versus individually. Take inventory of your children this week. Ask the Lord to reveal to you who they are in Him. Ask him to show you how to parent them according to his plan for them, not your own.

Prayer for Children (Protect, Nurture, Praise)

Heavenly Father,

We thank you for the blessing of children in our lives. We give you praise and glory for the joy and light that they bring to our lives.

We ask that you would help us to always remember the importance of cherishing and protecting these little ones, created in your image. Help us to love them and nurture them, to provide for their needs, both physical and spiritual.

We ask that you would be a shield of protection around our children, that you would keep them from harm and danger. Guide them in their growth and development, and help them to make wise decisions. Fill their hearts with peace and joy, and provide for their needs.

We also ask for your help in teaching our children to love and honor you. Help us to raise them in a way that pleases you, and to create an environment where they can thrive.

We pray these things in the name of Jesus. Amen.

Prayer for Parents: (Love, Strength, Wisdom)

Father God,

We come to You today on behalf of all parents around the world. We ask that You would give them the strength to face each day and the courage to make hard decisions. Help them to be good role models and provide a loving and nurturing environment for their children.

Lord, give them Your peace and rest as they take on the role of parenthood. Give them patience and wisdom as they strive to teach their children Your ways and to raise them up in righteousness.

Thank You for all the parents who are doing their best for their families. May this prayer be a reminder to them that You are with them every step of the way.

In Jesus' Name, Amen.

Practical Application

Write a targeted prayer for your child. If you have more than one child, write an individual prayer for each. Ask God to show you what to pray for beyond what you see. Use the prayer examples as jumpstarts.

_____

_____

_____

_____

_____

_____

_____

_____

_____

_____

_____

_____

_____

_____

Chapter Seven

CHILDREN PRAYER STRATEGIES

If you train your children to anything,
train them, at least, to a habit of prayer.
—J C RYLE

Oftentimes children are left out when it comes to prayer. Culturally, they are given the minimum expectations such as learning the Our Father Prayer or Saying Grace over their meals. However, in this season it is vital that we teach our children how to pray. We must understand that there is no junior Holy Spirit. Once our children have received Jesus Christ as their Savior, they are now able to have an intimate relationship with him. This means that they have access to every spiritual gift in the lives of the believer.

First we must teach children the power of prayer and why it is important. Talk about how prayer is a way to communicate with God and thank him for the blessings in our lives. Ensure that they truly understand that they have access to God. Encourage children to pray every day. Set aside a specific time for prayer each day, such as in the morning before school or before bed at night. Create prayer charts that help them to remember to pray.

Use the following teaching points with your children:

1. Teach children the power of prayer and why it is important. Explain to them that prayer is a way to communicate with God and thank him for the blessings in our lives. Discuss the power of prayer and how it can help us feel closer to God and gain peace in our lives.

2. Encourage children to pray every day. Show them how to set aside a specific time for prayer each day, such as in the morning before school or before bed at night. Discuss the importance of taking time out to pray every day and how it can help them focus on God's presence and be still.

3. Teach children to pray with sincerity and humility. Remind them to talk to God as if he were a loving friend. Explain how prayer is not about seeking glory from God, but rather about expressing our needs and desires, seeking guidance and thanksgiving.

4. Encourage children to pray for others, not just themselves. Teach them to pray for those in need, such as those who are sick, hungry, or suffering. Explain to them that prayer can be a powerful tool for helping others, and it is important to always be mindful of others and their needs.

5. Give children prayer books and other resources to help them learn how to pray. Provide them with books that contain prayers

and scripture to help them learn and understand the power of prayer.

6. Lead by example. Show children how to pray by praying yourself. Let them see you praying and explain to them why it is important.

7. Celebrate answered prayers. Help children to recognize how God has answered their prayers and thank him for it. Talk to them about how it is important to celebrate when prayers are answered and to give thanks for the good things that happen. Have them create prayer journals so that they can track their answered prayers.

Practical Application

Write a prayer plan for your child or children. Include teaching, application and times.

_____

_____

_____

_____

_____

_____

_____

_____

_____

_____

_____

_____

_____

Chapter Eight
CORPORATE PRAYER

A house divided, even in corporate prayer, cannot stand.
—PROPHETESS KISHA CEPHUS

T his final chapter focuses on what I believe to be the heart of God concerning the church, the ecclesia. The church has been upgraded spiritually from what has been considered the norm. The pandemic caused many pastors and churches to complete mandatory inventory on the effectiveness of their ministries. Yet even in the period of grace many did not heed the warning to transition. Now, we are in harvest season. This means that God is calling for the church to come higher in the place of prayer. Prophetically, God is raising up churches who will hearken to the call of prayer. This includes an uprising of prayer hubs, prayer ministries, prayer schools, and prayer revivals. I even see by way of the spirit where there will be seasons where the traditional praise service will be replaced with prayer service prior to the word being released.

Those who align with the shift need to also ensure that they understand the concept of corporate prayer. Oftentimes when it is time for prayer in a church service, one person is responsible for praying over the microphone. Now this prayer can take on multiple forms based on the denomination. I have seen leaders who begin to pray for their personal children. I have seen others who begin to complain in prayer. Then there is the charismatic leader that prays in tongues the entire time. In order for corporate prayer to be effective, unity must be restored to the church. What does this mean? Acts 2:1-4, "And when the day of Pentecost was fully come, they were all with one accord in one place. And suddenly there came a sound from heaven as of a rushing mighty wind, and it filled all the house where they were sitting. And there appeared unto them cloven tongues like as of fire, and it sat upon each of them. And they were all filled with the Holy Ghost, and began to speak with other tongues, as the Spirit gave them utterance." The converts in Acts all were obedient to the directions of Jesus prior to his ascension. They were in unity physically, mentally, and spiritually. This was the perfect recipe for a mighty move of God. This is what God wants to do with the 21st Century church.

Corporate prayer just like all other prayers mentioned in this book require preparation and instruction. As a matter of fact, because this involves multiple people, it is vital that the instructions are clear, specific and in order with the word of God. Matthew 18:18-20 (ESV) says, "Verily I say unto you, Whatsoever ye shall bind on earth shall be bound in heaven: and whatsoever ye shall loose on earth shall be loosed in heaven. Again I say unto you, That if two of you shall agree on earth as touching anything that they shall ask, it shall be done for them of my Father which is in heaven. For where two or three are gathered together in my name, there am I in the midst of them." This scripture is the foundation for corporate prayer. Whatever we pray together in agreement shall manifest. How powerful is that? This is why the enemy fights the prayer ministries and intercessors in the church. For if the church would ever walk into the power of the corporate prayer assignment, we would see a manifestation of the power and glory of God like never before.

Corporate prayer should never be centered around one individual. Now this doesn't mean that one individual can not facilitate. But the leader should be including the group in prayer. Remember, the purpose of corporate prayer is for a group of believers to come together unified in word, purpose, spirit, and power. Everyone in the church should be trained in the pattern of prayer for the house. This should be modeled after Jesus' prayer. This includes adoration, honor, recognizing the sovereignty of God, thanksgiving, and repentance. In addition, corporate prayer points should be included based on the vision of the house or the purpose of the prayer meeting. The person leading the prayer must bring the group into the prayer points by announcing them. Encourage the believers to pray along with you as you are praying throughout the time.

As I said, corporate prayer must have a strategy especially in altar nights or prayer meetings. During these times, corporate intercession takes place. Therefore, it's vital that the targets are hit in prayer. There should be structures and guidelines in place that all involved are aware of.

1. Psalm 133:1-3 - "Behold, how good and pleasant it is when brothers dwell in unity! It is like the precious oil on the head, running down on the beard, on the beard of Aaron, running down on the collar of his robes! It is like the dew of Hermon,

which falls on the mountains of Zion! For there the Lord has commanded the blessing, life forevermore."

2. Philippians 2:1-4 - "So if there is any encouragement in Christ, if any comfort from love, if any participation in the Spirit, if any affection and sympathy, complete my joy by being of the same mind, having the same love, being in full accord and of one mind. Do nothing from selfish ambition or conceit, but in humility count others more significant than yourselves. Let each of you look not only to his own interests, but also to the interests of others."

3. 1 Thessalonians 5:16-18 - "Rejoice always, pray without ceasing, give thanks in all circumstances; for this is the will of God in Christ Jesus for you."

4. Ephesians 6:18 - "Praying at all times in the Spirit, with all prayer and supplication. To that end keep alert with all perseverance, making supplication for all the saints."

5. Colossians 1:9-12 - "And so, from the day we heard, we have not ceased to pray for you, asking that you may be filled with the knowledge of his will in all spiritual wisdom and understanding, so as to walk in a manner worthy of the Lord, fully pleasing to him, bearing fruit in every good work and increasing in the knowledge of God. May you be strengthened with all power, according to his glorious might, for all endurance and patience with joy."

6. 1 Timothy 2:1-4 - "First of all, then, I urge that supplications, prayers, intercessions, and thanksgivings be made for all people, for kings and all who are in high positions, that we may lead a peaceful and quiet life, godly and dignified in every way.

This is good, and it is pleasing in the sight of God our Savior, who desires all people to be saved and to come to the knowledge of the truth."

7. Matthew 18:19-20 - "Again I say to you, if two of you agree on earth about anything they ask, it will be done for them by my Father in heaven. For where two or three are gathered in my name, there am I among them."

8. 2 Chronicles 7:14 - "If my people who are called by my name humble themselves, and pray and seek my face and turn from their wicked ways, then I will hear from heaven and will forgive their sin and heal their land."

9. Isaiah 56:7 - "These I will bring to my holy mountain, and make them joyful in my house of prayer; their burnt offerings and their sacrifices will be accepted on my altar; for my house shall be called a house of prayer for all peoples."

10. Psalm 5:3 - "O Lord, in the morning you hear my voice; in the morning I prepare a sacrifice for you and watch."

11. 1 John 5:14-15 - "And this is the confidence that we have toward him, that if we ask anything according to his will he hears us. And if we know that he hears us in whatever we ask, we know that we have the requests that we have asked of him."

12. Matthew 6:9-13 - "Pray then like this: 'Our Father in heaven, hallowed be your name. Your kingdom come, your will be done, on earth as it is in heaven. Give us this day our daily bread, and forgive us our debts, as we also have forgiven our debtors. And lead us not into temptation, but deliver us from evil.'"

Practical Application

Write a corporate prayer plan for your church, ministry, or group. Reflect on outcomes from bringing alignment to corporate prayer.

_____

_____

_____

_____

_____

_____

_____

_____

_____

_____

_____

_____

_____

Conclusion

Prayer is an essential part of our daily lives. We must take time each day to pray and open ourselves up to God's will. Although praying can be intimidating and overwhelming, it is important to remember that we have direct access to our Father who is Creator God. We should use different types of prayers to be able to talk to God in a way that is meaningful to us. Ultimately, prayer should be used to develop a deeper connection and understanding of God. As we practice and become more comfortable with prayer, we will find that it becomes a part of our daily routine and helps us to go deeper in our relationship with Him.

As the Bible says, "Rejoice always, pray without ceasing, give thanks in all circumstances; for this is the will of God in Christ Jesus for you" (1 Thessalonians 5:16-18). Prayer is a way of connecting with God and seeking His guidance and direction. As Saint Augustine said, "Pray as though everything depended on God. Work as though everything depended on you." We can be confident that when we pray, God will be faithful to answer our prayers in His perfect way and in His perfect time.

Addendum

RESOURCES FOR PRAYER

SCRIPTURES ON PRAYER

1. "Ask, and it will be given to you; seek, and you will find; knock, and it will be opened to you." - Matthew 7:7
2. "Be anxious for nothing, but in everything by prayer and supplication, with thanksgiving, let your requests be made known to God." - Philippians 4:6
3. "If you abide in me, and my words abide in you, ask whatever you wish, and it will be done for you." - John 15:7
4. "And this is the confidence that we have toward him, that if we ask anything according to his will, he hears us." - 1 John 5:14
5. "Continue steadfastly in prayer, being watchful in it with thanksgiving." - Colossians 4:2
6. "Pray without ceasing." - 1 Thessalonians 5:17
7. "Therefore I tell you, whatever you ask in prayer, believe that you have received it, and it will be yours." - Mark 11:24
8. "Likewise the Spirit helps us in our weakness. For we do not know what to pray for as we ought, but the Spirit himself intercedes for us with groanings too deep for words." - Romans 8:26
9. "And when you pray, do not heap up empty phrases as the Gentiles do, for they think that they will be heard for their many words." - Matthew 6:7
10. "But I say to you who hear, Love your enemies, do good to those who hate you, bless those who curse you, pray for those who abuse you." - Luke 6:27-28
11. "But when you pray, go into your room and shut the door and pray to your Father who is in secret. And your Father who sees in secret will reward you." - Matthew 6:6
12. "Is anyone among you suffering? Let him pray. Is anyone cheerful? Let him sing praise." - James 5:13
13. "Confess your sins to each other and pray for each other so that you may be healed. The earnest prayer of a righteous person has great power and produces wonderful results." -James 5:16 -
14. "Don't worry about anything; instead, pray about everything. Tell God what you need, and thank him for all he has done. Then you will experience God's peace, which exceeds anything we can understand. His peace will guard your hearts and minds as you live in Christ Jesus."-Philippians 4:6-7 -
15. "But when you pray, go away by yourself, shut the door behind you, and pray to your Father in private. Then your Father, who sees everything, will reward you." - Matthew 6:6
16. "Devote yourselves to prayer with an alert mind and a thankful heart." - Colossians 4:2
17. "Always be joyful. Never stop praying. Be thankful in all circumstances, for this is God's will for you who belong to Christ Jesus." - 1 Thessalonians 5:16-18

Below is an example Prayer Point created using scriptures 1 and 2.

Father God, I'm coming to you because I need provision for _____, your Word says to ask and it shall be given and to be anxious for nothing but in everything by prayer and supplication. So I come to you asking that if it's your will, you will make a way for _____.

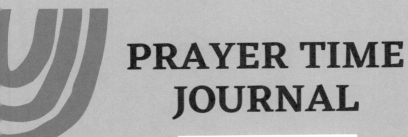

PRAYER TIME JOURNAL

DATE:

PRAYER TARGET:

SCRIPTURES:

WHAT DID YOU LEARN FROM THE SCRIPTURES ?

- ---
- ---
- ---
- ---

WHAT IS GOD SAYING BY WAY OF HOLY SPIRIT?

PRAYER TIME JOURNAL

DATE:

PRAYER TARGET:

SCRIPTURES:

WHAT DID YOU LEARN FROM THE SCRIPTURES ?

- ---
- ---
- ---
- ---

WHAT IS GOD SAYING BY WAY OF HOLY SPIRIT?

PRAYER TIME JOURNAL

DATE:

PRAYER TARGET:

SCRIPTURES:

WHAT DID YOU LEARN FROM THE SCRIPTURES ?

- ....
- ....
- ....
- ....

WHAT IS GOD SAYING BY WAY OF HOLY SPIRIT?

....

....

....

....

PRAYER TIME JOURNAL

DATE:

PRAYER TARGET:

SCRIPTURES:

WHAT DID YOU LEARN FROM THE SCRIPTURES ?

- ---
- ---
- ---
- ---

WHAT IS GOD SAYING BY WAY OF HOLY SPIRIT?

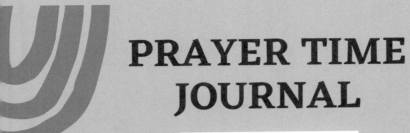

PRAYER TIME JOURNAL

DATE:

PRAYER TARGET:

SCRIPTURES:

WHAT DID YOU LEARN FROM THE SCRIPTURES ?

- --
- --
- --
- --

WHAT IS GOD SAYING BY WAY OF HOLY SPIRIT?

PRAYER TIME JOURNAL

DATE:

PRAYER TARGET:

SCRIPTURES:

WHAT DID YOU LEARN FROM THE SCRIPTURES ?

- --
- --
- --
- --

WHAT IS GOD SAYING BY WAY OF HOLY SPIRIT?

PRAYER TIME JOURNAL

DATE:

PRAYER TARGET:

SCRIPTURES:

WHAT DID YOU LEARN FROM THE SCRIPTURES ?

- ---
- ---
- ---
- ---

WHAT IS GOD SAYING BY WAY OF HOLY SPIRIT?

PRAYER TIME
JOURNAL

DATE:

PRAYER TARGET:

SCRIPTURES:

WHAT DID YOU LEARN FROM THE SCRIPTURES ?

- _____
- _____
- _____
- _____

WHAT IS GOD SAYING BY WAY OF HOLY SPIRIT?

_____

_____

_____

_____

PRAYER TIME JOURNAL

DATE:

PRAYER TARGET:

SCRIPTURES:

WHAT DID YOU LEARN FROM THE SCRIPTURES ?

- --
- --
- --
- --

WHAT IS GOD SAYING BY WAY OF HOLY SPIRIT?

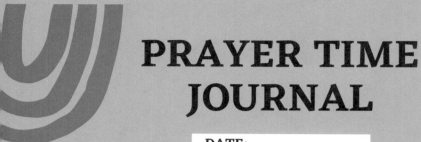

PRAYER TIME JOURNAL

DATE:

PRAYER TARGET:

SCRIPTURES:

WHAT DID YOU LEARN FROM THE SCRIPTURES ?

- --
- --
- --
- --

WHAT IS GOD SAYING BY WAY OF HOLY SPIRIT?

Rochelle Scott

Motivational Speaker, Coach, Shiftologist , & Podcast Host

Rochelle is a Wife, Mother, Prophet, Preacher, Coach, Mentor, Consultant, Educator, Motivational Speaker and Spiritual Advisor. Rochelle's desire is to shift Cultures and dismantle detrimental systems in order for people to come into alignment with their God given purpose! Rochelle is called to multidimensionally tear down and to build. Rochelle is the podcast host for "I Am a Shifter!" Rochelle walks ambidextrously in the fivefold ministry and is #mentoredbyJesus !

SIGNATURE TOPICS

✓ Kingdom Leadership 101

✓ Shiftology

✓ Who Am I? (The Identity Crisis)

✓ Where's the Church?

✓ Restoring the Family

✓ The WHOLE Woman

Get in Touch!

Please feel free to reach out for any questions.

✉ rwashingtonscott@gmail.com
⬚ Rochelle Washington Scott
🌐 https://rochellescott.my.canva.site/
Ⓕ Kingdom Reset , Culture Reset